Thank You

First of all a big **THANK YOU** for purchasing my very first book!
When I left my career as a research scientist, to spend more
time with my daughter, I started to miss helping students fulfil
their potential and the colourful world of biology that had been
a part of my life for so long.

Soon enough, I found myself doodling on pieces of paper, trying
to keep in touch with the subject that I love. Taking inspiration
from the online study and bujo communities, I began to share
my work, my daughter's playroom became my make-shift office
and Doctor Me Clever was born.

This book has been lovingly hand-designed for you and I hope it
allows you to see biology in a new light.

Dream Big.
Wishing you the very best of luck with your revision.

Laura.

Dedication

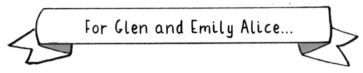

For Glen and Emily Alice...

Thank you to my daughter Emily for her Crayola comments and daily inspiration.

Thank you to my husband Glen, for supporting my change in career and the late nights that came with it.

Thank you to my mum for the hours of childcare she has so kindly provided. Thank you dad for putting up with the toy hurricane in your lounge!

Thank you to my sister Dr Sarah Wetherill, whose medical writing skills came in very handy!

You're all stars.

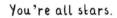

Copyright
Information

DOCTOR ME CLEVER

CONTENTS & TRACKER

Each time you revise a section, put your mark on a circle!

CELLS

Cell = the basic structural and functional unit of all living organisms.

LIVING ORGANISMS

..can be divided into..

EUKARYOTES ..OR.. **PROKARYOTES**

(Multicellular organisms)   (Unicellular organisms)

Complex cells   ..these organisms are made up of either..   Simple cell

EUKARYOTIC CELLS ..OR.. **A PROKARYOTIC CELL**

DNA contained within a nucleus.      The defining feature?   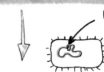   DNA floating free in the cytoplasm.

HAVE A NUCLEUS   NO NUCLEUS

examples

example

TYPICAL ANIMAL CELL   **TYPICAL PLANT CELL**   **TYPICAL BACTERIAL CELL**

Permanent, large vacuole

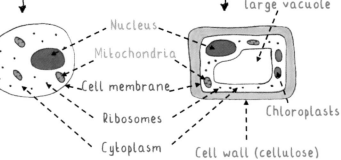

Nucleus
Mitochondria
Cell membrane
Ribosomes
Cytoplasm
Chloroplasts
Cell wall (cellulose)

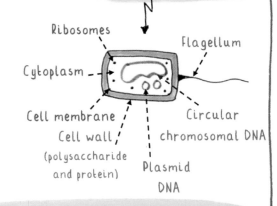

Ribosomes
Cytoplasm
Cell membrane
Cell wall (polysaccharide and protein)
Flagellum
Circular chromosomal DNA
Plasmid DNA

SUBCELLULAR STRUCTURES

Some subcellular structures are common to animal, plant and bacterial cells, others can only be found in plant or bacterial cells.

Prokaryotic cells are much SMALLER than eukaryotic cells.

Remember eukaryote/prokaryote describes the organism. Eukaryotic/prokaryotic describes the cell type.

1

SUBCELLULAR STRUCTURES

> SUBCELLULAR STRUCTURES are features of a cell that have a particular function.

For your exam you will need to know the subcellular structures that are found in animal, plant and bacterial cells. You will also be expected to know the function of each subcellular structure.

COMMON TO ANIMAL, PLANT and BACTERIAL CELLS

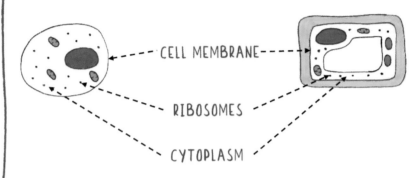

CELL MEMBRANE

RIBOSOMES

CYTOPLASM

> There are 3 subcellular structures common to animal, plant and bacterial cells.

CYTOPLASM: The **gel-like substance containing enzymes.** This is where most of the cell's **chemical reactions take place.**

RIBOSOMES: Where **translation** of genetic material occurs, resulting in **protein synthesis** i.e. where proteins are made.

CELL MEMBRANE: Barrier that **holds the cell together** and is responsible for controlling which **substances pass in and out** of the cell.

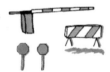

UNIQUE TO ANIMAL and PLANT CELLS

NUCLEUS: Where the **genetic material,** that controls the cell's activities, is **stored** as chromosomes.

> Bacterial cells DO NOT contain mitochondria or a nucleus.

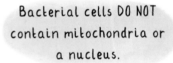

MITOCHONDRIA: Where the **energy,** that the cell needs to function, is **released in respiration.**

> Bacterial cells have genetic material (DNA) but it is not contained within a nucleus.

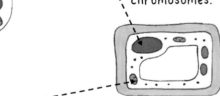

SUBCELLULAR STRUCTURES

UNIQUE TO PLANT CELLS

There are 3 subcellular structures unique to plant cells.

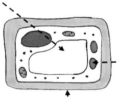

PERMANENT, LARGE VACUOLE: Filled with **cell sap** (a weak solution of sugar and salt), the large vacuole helps to support the plant cell and keep it **turgid**.

CHLOROPLASTS: Where **photosynthesis** occurs. Chloroplasts **contain** the green pigment **chlorophyll**.

CELL WALL (CELLULOSE): Made from the carbohydrate **cellulose**, the cell wall is rigid, providing the plant cell with **structure and strength**.

UNIQUE TO BACTERIAL CELLS

There are 4 subcellular structures unique to bacterial cells.

CIRCULAR CHROMOSOMAL DNA: A single, **large**, **circular piece of DNA** that controls the cell's activities and replication. This **DNA floats freely** in the cytoplasm and is **NOT contained within a nucleus**.

FLAGELLUM: A **rotating, whip-like tail** that allows the bacterial cell to **move towards nutrients and away from toxins**. Bacterial cells can have more than one flagellum (**flagella**).

PLASMID DNA: **Small loops of DNA** that contain **extra genetic information** e.g. antibiotic resistance genes. They can be passed between bacteria.

CELL WALL

(POLYSACCHARIDE AND PROTEIN): Made from **polysaccharide and protein**, the cell wall provides **structure** to the bacterial cell.

SUMMARY of SUBCELLULAR STRUCTURES

Where can I find each subcellular structure?

KEY

- Animal Cell
- Plant Cell
- Bacterial Cell

- Cytoplasm
- Cell Membrane
- Ribosomes
- Mitochondria
- Nucleus
- Cell Wall (cellulose)
- Chloroplasts
- Permanent, Large Vacuole
- Circular Chromosomal DNA
- Plasmid DNA
- Flagellum
- Cell Wall (polysaccharide & protein)

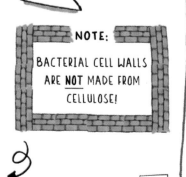

NOTE:

BACTERIAL CELL WALLS ARE **NOT** MADE FROM CELLULOSE!

TYPICAL vs. SPECIALISED CELLS

TYPICAL CELLS are a generalisation and describe the **basic features** common to an **"average"** cell belonging to a particular organism.

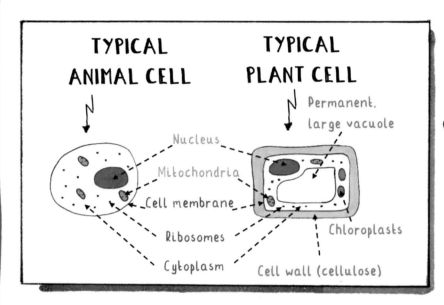

TYPICAL ANIMAL CELL

TYPICAL PLANT CELL

Nucleus

Mitochondria

Cell membrane

Ribosomes

Cytoplasm

Permanent, large vacuole

Chloroplasts

Cell wall (cellulose)

However, **MULTICELLULAR ORGANISMS** such as **PLANTS & ANIMALS** contain **many types of cells** that have **different roles** within an organism. These cells are called **SPECIALISED CELLS**.

SPECIALISED CELLS are **adapted** to carry out a **specific function**.

▷ Most **SPECIALISED CELLS** contain **all the basic features of a typical cell**, but they have **extra structures** (or **adaptations**) that allow them to do a specific job.

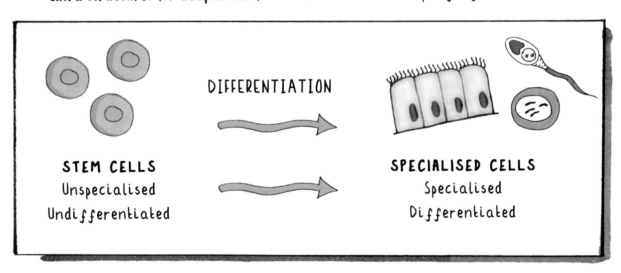

DIFFERENTIATION

STEM CELLS
Unspecialised
Undifferentiated

SPECIALISED CELLS
Specialised
Differentiated

Embryonic stem cells can **differentiate** into any specialised cell type.

Nearly all cells in the human body are specialised to carry out a particular function.

4

SPECIALISED CELLS

1.   SPECIALISED FOR SEXUAL REPRODUCTION.

▷ **Adapted** to **transport** the male's **DNA** to the female's egg.

☆ ADAPTATIONS ☆

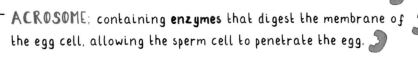

ACROSOME; containing **enzymes** that digest the membrane of the egg cell, allowing the sperm cell to penetrate the egg.

HAPLOID NUCLEUS; containing the **male's half** of the **chromosomes** needed to make a whole body cell.

MIDDLE SECTION; containing lots of **mitochondria**, required to produce the **energy** needed (via respiration) for the sperm cell to swim to the egg.

LONG TAIL; allowing the sperm cell to **swim** to the egg.

2.  SPECIALISED FOR SEXUAL REPRODUCTION.

▷ **Adapted** to **hold** the female's **DNA**.
▷ **Adapted** to **nourish** the **embryo** during the early stages of development.

☆ ADAPTATIONS ☆

HAPLOID NUCLEUS; containing the **female's half** of the **chromosomes** needed to make a whole body cell.

NUTRIENT-RICH CYTOPLASM; that **nourishes** the developing embryo.

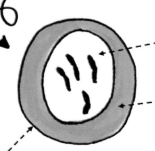

CELL MEMBRANE; that **changes structure**, after fertilisation, to prevent any more sperm cells penetrating the egg. This ensures that offspring contain the **right amount of DNA** (and no extra DNA, from additional sperm cells).

 All sperm and egg cells, regardless of the animal of origin, contain half the number of chromosomes found in a "normal" body cell. Sperm and egg cells contain one chromosome from each chromosome pair.

SPECIALISED CELLS

CILIATED EPITHELIAL CELLS

SPECIALISED FOR MOVING MATERIALS.

▷ **Adapted** to line the surfaces of organs and **move substances** in **one direction.**

☆ ADAPTATION ☆

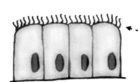

CILIA are hair-like structures found on the top of the ciliated epithelial cell. They "beat" to move materials in one direction.

Example

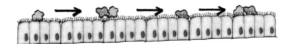

A lining of ciliated epithelial cells.

▷ Your **airways** are **lined** with ciliated epithelial cells (a type of ciliated cell).

▷ Their function is to **trap particles** from the air that you breathe and help to **move them** up to your mouth in **MUCUS.**

▷ Once in your mouth, the mucus can be swallowed, **preventing** the potentially **harmful particles reaching your lungs.**

💡 Note: Ciliated epithelial cells also line the fallopian tubes.

SUMMARY - SPECIALISED CELLS

SPECIALISED CELL	FUNCTION	☆ ADAPTATIONS ☆
Sperm 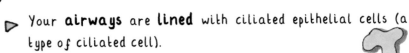	Transports the male's DNA to the female's egg.	Long **tail**, mitochondria-rich **middle section**, **acrosome** and haploid **nucleus.**
Egg	Holds the female's DNA and **nourishes** the embryo during the early stages of development.	Haploid **nucleus**, nutrient rich **cytoplasm** and structural change in cell **membrane.**
Ciliated Epithelial Cells 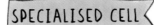	Moves materials/substances.	Hair-like **cilia.**

MICROSCOPY: BASICS

To make bigger.

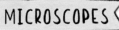 **MICROSCOPES** use **lenses** to magnify and increase the resolution of images.

The resolution of a microscope is how well it distinguishes between two points that are close together i.e. the degree of detail.

● = actual size of the blue dot magnified below...

Microscopes are used to view samples that may not be visible to the naked eye.

Microscopes allow us to resolve detail that cannot be seen by the naked eye.

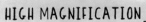 **HIGH MAGNIFICATION**

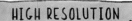 **HIGH RESOLUTION**

High

Image is **much bigger** than the actual size.

 **MAGNIFICATION**

Image is **several times bigger** than the actual size.

Low

High

Image is **clearer**.
Image is **more detailed**.

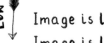 **RESOLUTION**

Image is **less clear**.
Image is **less detailed**.

Low

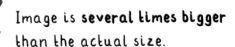 **LOW MAGNIFICATION**

LOW RESOLUTION

 **A brief HISTORY of MICROSCOPY**

 The **LIGHT** microscope was **invented.** ⇒ → 1590s

Uses a light source and glass lenses.

Uses electrons and electromagnetic lenses.

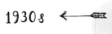 1930s ← The **ELECTRON** microscope was invented.

 7

MICROSCOPY: BASICS

LIGHT vs. ELECTRON MICROSCOPES

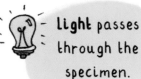 **Light** passes through the specimen.

 Lower magnification.

Electrons pass through the specimen.

 Higher magnification.

Light Microscope

Electron Microscope

MAIN DIFFERENCES

Can view **living** cells or organisms.

Lower resolution; can distinguish between organelles.

Specimen must be **dead**.

Higher resolution; can distinguish between internal structures of organelles.

ADVANTAGES & DISADVANTAGES

LIGHT MICROSCOPE

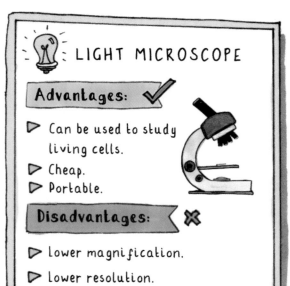

Advantages: ✔
▷ Can be used to study living cells.
▷ Cheap.
▷ Portable.

Disadvantages: ✖
▷ Lower magnification.
▷ Lower resolution.

ELECTRON MICROSCOPE

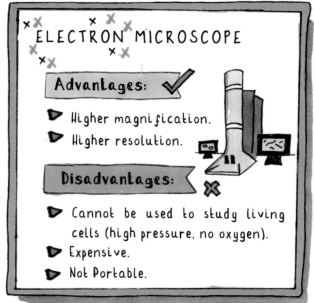

Advantages: ✔
▷ Higher magnification.
▷ Higher resolution.

Disadvantages:
▷ Cannot be used to study living cells (high pressure, no oxygen).
▷ Expensive.
▷ Not Portable.

Q. **HOW** did the invention of the **ELECTRON MICROSCOPE** change research?

A. The electron microscope allowed scientists to study **smaller specimens** with **more clarity and in greater detail**. This led to a **greater understanding** of how cells and their subcellular structures work.

MICROSCOPY: BASICS

SCALE AND SIZE

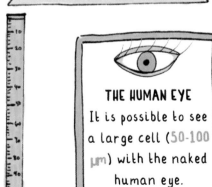

THE HUMAN EYE

It is possible to see a large cell (50-100 μm) with the naked human eye.

LIGHT MICROSCOPE

Max resolution of 200 nm.
Max magnification of X2,000.
Used to study large organelles such as nuclei.

ELECTRON MICROSCOPE

Max resolution of 50 pm.
Max magnification of X10,000,000.
Used to study tiny subcellular structures such as ribosomes and plasmid DNA.

METER	CENTIMETER	MILLIMETER	MICROMETER	NANOMETER	PICOMETER
10^0 m	10^{-2} m	10^{-3} m	10^{-6} m	10^{-9} m	10^{-12} m
1 m	0.01 m	0.001 m	0.000001 m	0.000000001 m	0.000000000001 m
	1/100 m	1/1,000 m	1/1,000,000 m	1/1,000,000,000 m	1/1,000,000,000,000 m
	1 cm	1 mm	1 μm	1 nm	1 pm
	Hundredth of a meter	Thousandth of a meter	Millionth of a meter	Billionth of a meter	Trillionth of a meter

How to convert the units..

 ÷100   ÷10 ÷1000 ÷1000 ÷1000

METER CENTIMETER MILLIMETER MICROMETER NANOMETER PICOMETER

X100 X10 X1000 X1000 X1000

SCALE BARS

A scale bar is a length, drawn on a magnified image that represents a convenient "actual length".

EXAMPLE

Draw a 50 μm scale bar on the image (D). The actual size of the specimen is 150 μm.

A. Measure the length of the image in mm (note this image is not to scale).

Divide the size of the image by the same number (3) to get the length of the scale bar you need to draw on the image (make sure the units are the same in A and D).

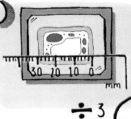

Size of image.

30 mm ÷3 10 mm

Drawn length of scale bar on image.

Actual size of specimen.

150 μm ÷3 50 μm

length the scale bar needs to represent.

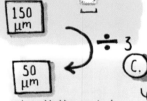

B. Fill in the actual size of the specimen.

Divide the actual size of the specimen (B) by the length the scale bar needs to represent (C) (make sure the units are the same in B and C). For this example the answer is 3.

C.

D.

9

MICROSCOPY: PRACTICAL

> INVESTIGATING BIOLOGICAL SPECIMENS USING A MICROSCOPE.

1. > PREPARE THE SPECIMEN SLIDE <

> METHOD <

PLANT CELLS (ONION CELLS)

A. > COLLECT SAMPLE <

▷ Use tweezers to peel a **thin layer of tissue** (epidermal cells) from the onion. It needs to be thin to allow **light to pass** through it.

tweezers

Thin layer
of onion

Onion   Microscope light

B. > TRANSFER AND STAIN <

▷ Pipette a **drop of water** onto the centre of a **clean slide**.

▷ Use tweezers to lay the sample on top of the water.

▷ Add a drop of IODINE to stain the cell walls and nuclei.

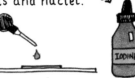

IODINE

ANIMAL CELLS (HUMAN CHEEK CELLS)

A. > COLLECT SAMPLE <

▷ **Swab** the inside of your **cheek** with a **clean cotton bud** to remove some cheek cells.

Cells on the
cotton bud

B. > TRANSFER AND STAIN <

▷ Pipette a **drop of water** onto the centre of a **clean slide**.

▷ **Transfer sample**, on the cotton bud, to the water.

▷ Add a drop of METHYLENE BLUE to **stain** the DNA in the nuclei.

MB

C. > SECURE <

▷ Using a **mounted needle**, place a **coverslip** at an **angle**, at one end of the specimen. **Gently lower** it over the specimen.

▷ Press down gently to **remove air bubbles**.

MICROSCOPY: PRACTICAL

INVESTIGATING BIOLOGICAL SPECIMENS USING A MICROSCOPE.

2. SET THE MICROSCOPE

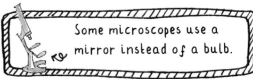
Some microscopes use a mirror instead of a bulb.

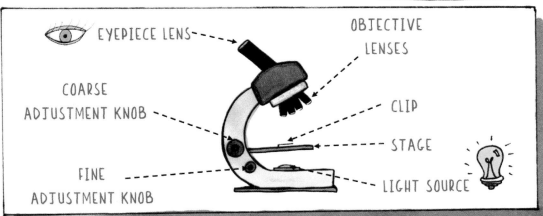

EYEPIECE LENS

OBJECTIVE LENSES

COARSE ADJUSTMENT KNOB

CLIP

STAGE

FINE ADJUSTMENT KNOB

LIGHT SOURCE

A. Use the CLIP to secure the slide on the STAGE.

B. Select the **lowest-powered** OBJECTIVE LENS.

C. Move the slide **upwards** to the OBJECTIVE LENS by **moving the** STAGE with the COARSE ADJUSTMENT KNOB.

D. Look through the EYEPIECE LENS and use the COARSE ADJUSTMENT KNOB to move the STAGE **downwards**. Stop when the specimen is **almost in focus.**

E. Use the FINE ADJUSTMENT KNOB to make the image **clear.**

3. MEASURE THE FIELD OF VIEW

NEED HIGHER MAGNIFICATION?

▷ Use a higher powered objective lens.

▷ Refocus using the adjustment knobs.

▷ Place **a clear ruler** on the stage and measure the **diameter** of the circular area that can be viewed down the microscope. This area is called the **FIELD OF VIEW (FOV).**

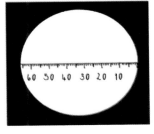

Increasing magnification

Decreasing FOV

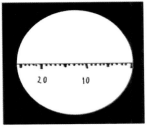

As the magnification increases the FOV decreases.

FOV = 66 mm

FOV = 26 mm

MICROSCOPY: PRACTICAL

INVESTIGATING BIOLOGICAL SPECIMENS USING A MICROSCOPE.

4. DRAW A SCIENTIFIC DIAGRAM

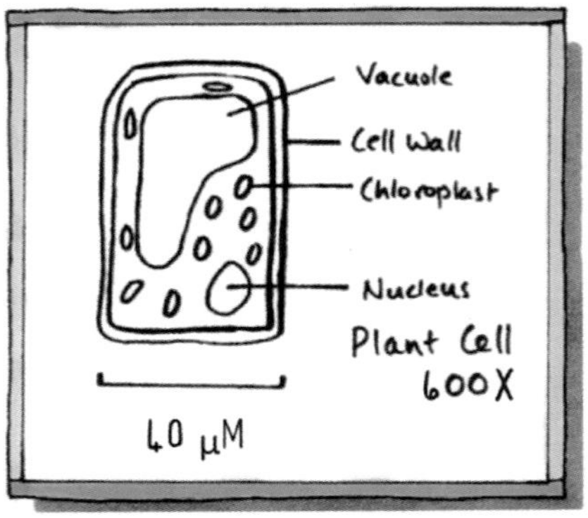

Outline the main features. Keep them in proportion.

½ Use half the space.

Do not use colour or shading.

Add a **scale bar**.

Use a **sharp pencil**.

NAME BADGE

Add the specimen name.

Plant Cell 600X
Vacuole
Cell Wall
Chloroplast
Nucleus
40 μM

Label using straight, unbroken lines that do not cross.

Add the magnification.

What will I see?

✓ Under a light microscope you will see;

▷ Cell Membrane
▷ Cytoplasm
▷ Nucleus
▷ Mitochondria (maybe)

Animal or plant cells

▷ Cell Wall (cellulose)
▷ Chloroplasts (maybe)
▷ Permanent vacuole (maybe)

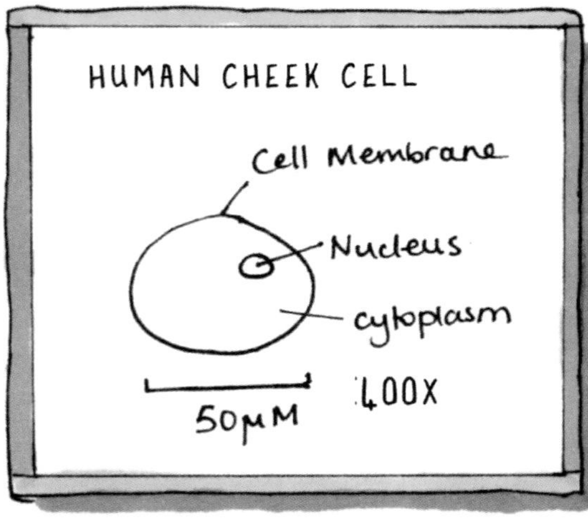

Plant cells only

HUMAN CHEEK CELL
Cell Membrane
Nucleus
cytoplasm
50μM   400X

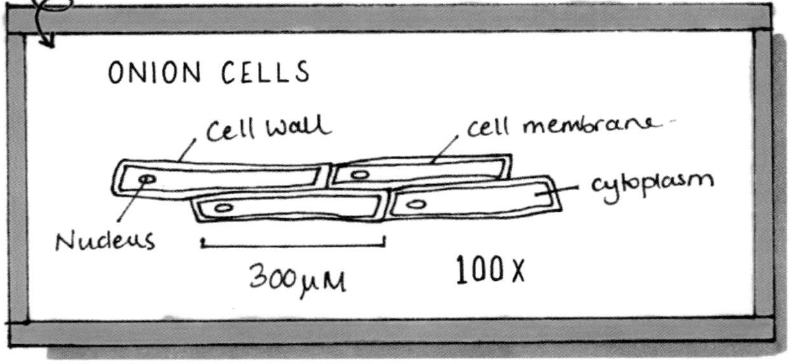

ONION CELLS
Cell Wall
cell membrane
cytoplasm
Nucleus
300μM   100X

✗ Under a light microscope you will **NOT** see;

▷ Ribosomes
▷ Internal structures of organelles.

MICROSCOPY: CALCULATIONS

CALCULATING TOTAL MAGNIFICATION

Each lens can **magnify** the image a certain number of times. This is known as the magnification **POWER of the lens** e.g. ten times (10X), sixty times (60X) etc...

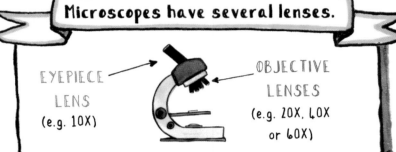

Microscopes have several lenses.

EYEPIECE LENS (e.g. 10X)

OBJECTIVE LENSES (e.g. 20X, 40X or 60X)

→ THERE ARE TWO EQUATIONS FOR CALCULATING TOTAL MAGNIFICATION.. ←

Equation #ONE

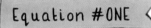   

The TOTAL MAGNIFICATION of an image can be calculated if you know the **POWERs** of the EYEPIECE LENS and the **OBJECTIVE LENS** being used.

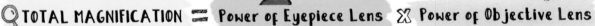 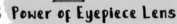

TOTAL MAGNIFICATION = Power of Eyepiece Lens ✗ Power of Objective Lens

EXAMPLE:

Power of Eyepiece Lens = 10X
Power of Objective Lens = 60X
Total Magnification = 10 ✗ 60 = 600
The TOTAL MAGNIFICATION is 600X

Equation #TWO

You can also calculate the TOTAL MAGNIFICATION (using the "I AM" triangle) if you are given the ACTUAL SIZE of the specimen and a magnified IMAGE of the sample to measure.

TOTAL MAGNIFICATION = Image Size ÷ Actual Size

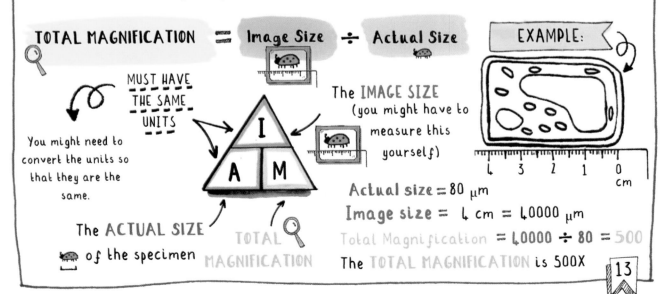

MUST HAVE THE SAME UNITS

You might need to convert the units so that they are the same.

The IMAGE SIZE (you might have to measure this yourself)

The ACTUAL SIZE of the specimen

TOTAL MAGNIFICATION

EXAMPLE:

Actual size = 80 μm
Image size = 4 cm = 40000 μm
Total Magnification = 40000 ÷ 80 = 500
The TOTAL MAGNIFICATION is 500X

ENZYMES: BASICS

ENZYMES are **BIOLOGICAL CATALYSTS** produced by living organisms.

They catalyse (CAUSE or ACCELERATE) chemical reactions.

Active Site: the part of the enzyme that **BINDS** to the substrate and **CATALYSES** the reaction. Its shape **COMPLEMENTS** the shape of the substrate.

Substrate: the MOLECULE that an ENZYME ACTS ON.

Enzyme
(remains **unchanged** and is **not used up** during the reaction)

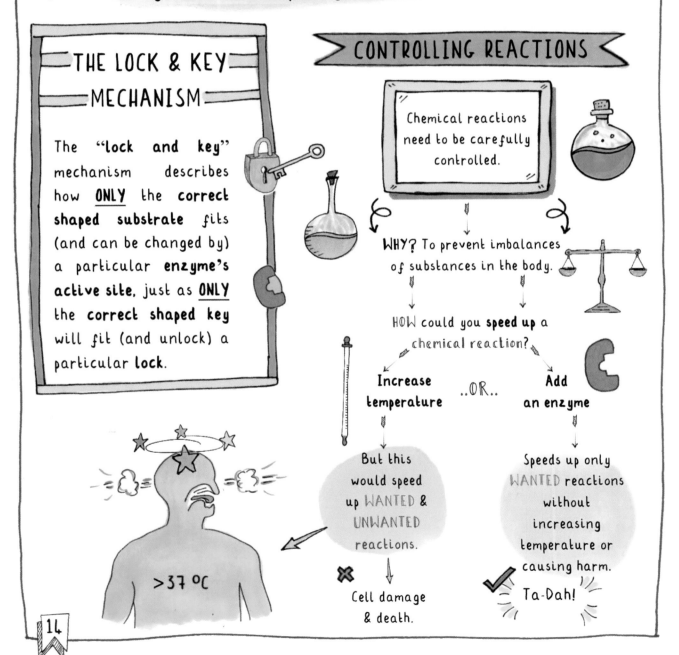

THE LOCK & KEY MECHANISM

The "**lock and key**" mechanism describes how **ONLY** the **correct shaped substrate** fits (and can be changed by) a particular **enzyme's active site**, just as **ONLY** the **correct shaped key** will fit (and unlock) a particular **lock**.

CONTROLLING REACTIONS

Chemical reactions need to be carefully controlled.

WHY? To prevent imbalances of substances in the body.

HOW could you **speed up** a chemical reaction?

Increase temperature   ..OR..   **Add an enzyme**

But this would speed up WANTED & UNWANTED reactions.

✗ Cell damage & death.

Speeds up only WANTED reactions without increasing temperature or causing harm. Ta-Dah! ✓

>37 °C

ENZYMES: BASICS

ENZYMES CAN..

..**BREAK DOWN** a substrate

..OR..

..**ADD** substrates **TOGETHER** (SYNTHESIS)

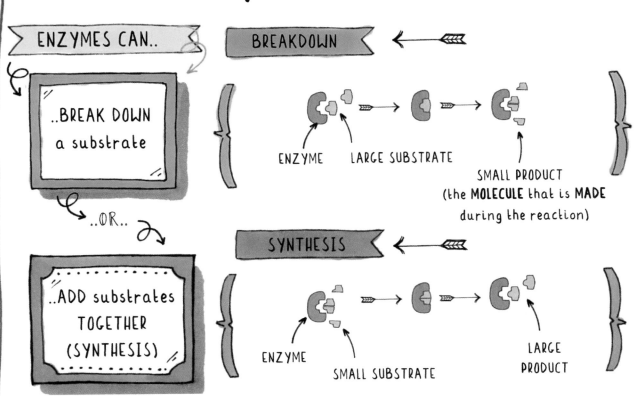

BREAKDOWN

ENZYME LARGE SUBSTRATE

SMALL PRODUCT
(the **MOLECULE** that is **MADE** during the reaction)

SYNTHESIS

ENZYME

SMALL SUBSTRATE

LARGE PRODUCT

DENATURATION

▷ **DENATURATION** is a **process** in which an enzyme **changes shape** and is **unbale to catalyse** its reaction.

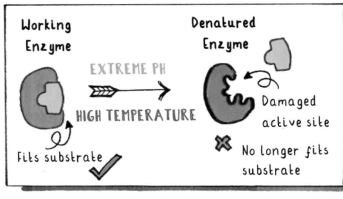

Working Enzyme

EXTREME PH

HIGH TEMPERATURE

Fits substrate ✓

Denatured Enzyme

Damaged active site

✗ No longer fits substrate

ENZYMES are **NEITHER DEAD** nor **ALIVE!**

▷ An enzyme **cannot "die"** or be **"killed"** because enzymes are not living organisms! Enzymes are **biological molecules** (proteins) made by living organisms.

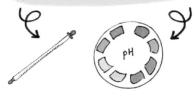

Denaturation is caused by **high temperature** or **extreme pH.**

▷ **HIGH TEMPERATURE** or EXTREME pH cause **bonds** in the **active site** of an enzyme to **break**, changing its **shape**.

▷ The **shape** of a **denatured enzyme's active site** is **no longer complementary** to the shape of the substrate and therefore the **enzyme** can no longer catalyse the reaction..

ENZYMES: RATE OF REACTION

RATE OF REACTION — The speed at which an enzyme converts its substrate to product.

≈ **THE RATE OF REACTION CAN BE AFFECTED BY 3 VARIABLES...** ≈

1. Substrate Concentration

▷ **LOWER** substrate concentration.

▷ **SLOWER** reaction rate.
▷ **FEWER** enzyme and substrate interactions per second.

Maximum reaction rate

All active sites full (saturation) and reaction rate cannot increase further.

Substrate concentration required to achieve maximum reaction rate.

Rate of Reaction (s⁻¹) vs *Substrate Concentration (M)*

▷ **HIGHER** substrate concentration.

▷ **FASTER** reaction rate.
▷ **MORE** enzyme and substrate interactions per second.

2. Temperature

Maximum reaction rate

Peak rate of reaction at the optimum temperature.

Reaction rate decreases as enzyme becomes denatured.

Rate of Reaction (s⁻¹) vs *Temperature (°C)* — Optimum temperature

Optimum temperature
▷ The temperature at which the enzyme works best.

EXTREME TEMPERATURE can **DENATURE ENZYMES**

At low temperatures, the enzyme and substrate have little energy, leading to a low rate of reaction.

3. pH

EXTREME pH can DENATURE ENZYMES

Optimum pH
▷ The pH at which the enzyme works best.

Maximum reaction rate

Peak rate of reaction at the optimum pH.

Reaction rate decreases as enzyme becomes denatured.

Rate of Reaction (s⁻¹) vs *pH* — Optimum pH

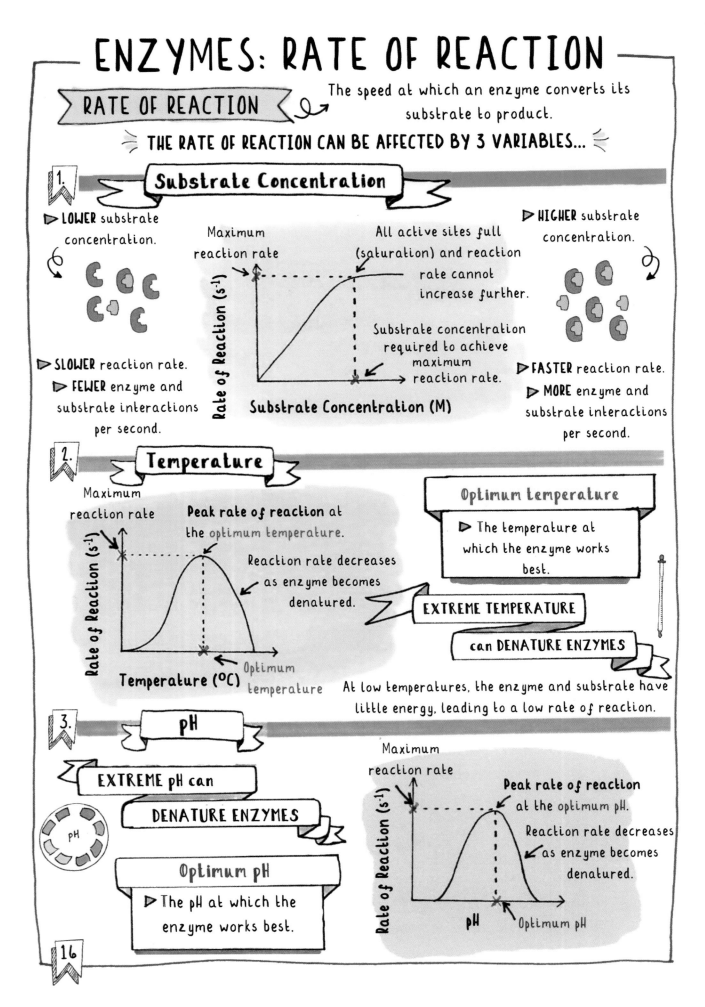

ENZYMES: PRACTICAL

How does pH affect the ability of amylase to break starch down into maltose?

ENZYMATIC REACTION ⟶   Starch   Amylase enzyme   Maltose

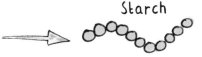

METHOD

1. SET UP

A.) Add **one drop of iodine** to **each well** of a spotting tile.

B.) Add **starch solution (S, 2 cm³)** to one boiling tube. Add **amylase solution (A, 2 cm³)** and **pH5 buffer (B, 1 cm³)** to another boiling tube. Heat to **35 °C**.

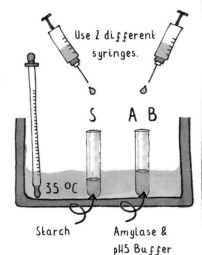

Use 2 different syringes.

35 °C

Starch   Amylase & pH5 Buffer

2. MIX & SAMPLE

C.) **Mix** both solutions into one boiling tube and place at **35 °C**. Start the stopwatch immediately.

SAB

D.) Add one **drop** of solution (SAB) to a single well containing iodine, **every 30 seconds (continuous sampling).**

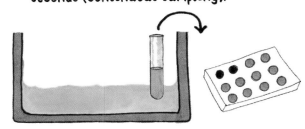

3. RECORD & REPEAT

E.) **Record** the **time** that corresponds to the **first well that remains orange-brown.** This is the time it takes for the substrate (starch) to be broken down.

pH	Time (s)
5	360
6	
7	
8	

F.) **Repeat** this experiment with buffers of **different pH values.**

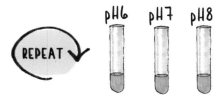

REPEAT   pH6 pH7 pH8

ENZYMES: PRACTICAL

THE REACTION IS COMPLETE WHEN THERE IS NO STARCH LEFT AND THE IODINE DOES NOT CHANGE COLOUR.

EXAMPLE

pH	Time (s)
5	360
6	270
7	120
8	270

Starch   Amylase enzyme   Maltose

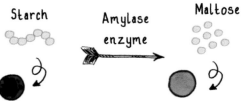

Solution turns Blue-Black. Positive for starch. Enzymatic reaction incomplete.

Solution remains Brown-Orange. Negative for starch. Enzymatic reaction complete.

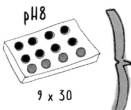

Note: Sample taken every 30 seconds.

pH5

pH6
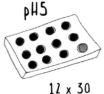

pH7
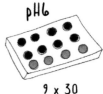

pH8
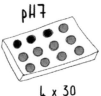

Reaction Completion Time

12 x 30	9 x 30	4 x 30	9 x 30
= 360 seconds	= 270 seconds	= 120 seconds	= 270 seconds

CALCULATING THE RATES OF REACTION:

RATES OF REACTION

For the amylase experiment, which DOES NOT measure a change in volume, use the following equation:

$$\text{Rate of the reaction (s}^{-1}) = 1000 \div \text{time (s)}$$

$$\frac{1000}{\text{⏱}}$$

pH5 $1000 \div 360 = 2.8 \text{ s}^{-1}$

pH6 $1000 \div 270 = 3.7 \text{ s}^{-1}$

pH7 $1000 \div 120 = 8.3 \text{ s}^{-1}$

pH8 $1000 \div 270 = 3.7 \text{ s}^{-1}$

For experiments that DO measure a change in volume use the following equation:

$$\text{Rate of reaction (cm}^3\text{s}^{-1}) = \text{volume change (cm}^3) \div \text{time (s)}$$

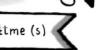
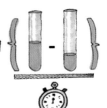

A FAIR TEST:

Variables that need to be controlled:

▷ Use the same volumes and concentrations of both the substrate (starch) and the enzyme (amylase) for each pH value tested.

▷ If using a Bunsen burner to keep the water warm, monitor the temperature of the water with a thermometer and keep it constant.

ENZYMES: BREAKDOWN

BREAKDOWN

Some enzymes break down large molecules into smaller molecules so that they can be used in GROWTH and other LIFE PROCESSES.

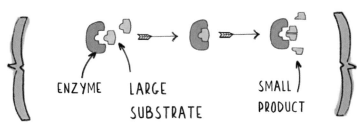

ENZYME   LARGE SUBSTRATE   SMALL PRODUCT

▷ LARGE MOLECULES = proteins, complex carbohydrates and lipids ◁
▷ SMALL MOLECULES = amino acids, simple sugars, glycerol and fatty acids ◁

LARGE Substrate	Enzyme(s)	SMALL Product(s)
⬇	⬇	⬇

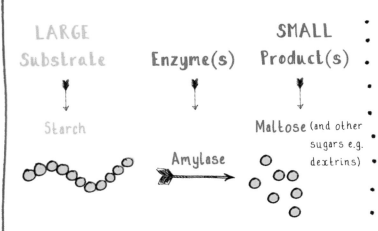

Starch → Amylase → Maltose (and other sugars e.g. dextrins)

CARBOHYDRASES break down **carbohydrates** into **simple sugars** e.g. AMYLASE (carbohydrase) converts **starch** (complex carbohydrate) into **maltose** (simple sugar).

Proteins → Proteases → Amino Acids

PROTEASES break down **proteins** into **amino acids**.

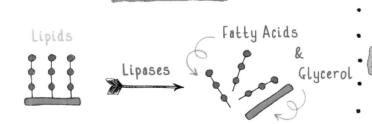

Lipids → Lipases → Fatty Acids & Glycerol

LIPASES break down **lipids** into **fatty acids and glycerol**.

Example in Plants

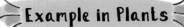

Plants use the large molecule **STARCH** to store energy.

Enzymes break starch down into **sugars** (small molecules).

Sugar is needed during **RESPIRATION** to generate **ENERGY**.

Example in Animals

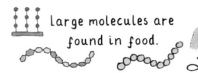

Large molecules are found in food.

Digestive enzymes break down **large molecules** into **smaller molecules**.

Smaller molecules can pass through the **walls of the digestive system** and are easily **absorbed** into the **bloodstream** and **cells**.

Here, they can be used by the body for **GROWTH** and other **LIFE PROCESSES**.

19

ENZYMES: SYNTHESIS

Some enzymes can synthesise (make) large molecules by adding smaller molecules together.

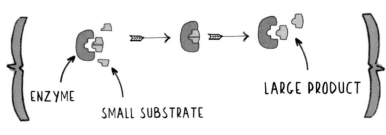

ENZYME   SMALL SUBSTRATE   LARGE PRODUCT

Organisms need to be able to synthesise large molecules such as proteins, complex carbohydrates and lipids.

SMALL Substrate	Enzyme(s)	LARGE Product
Amino Acids	Several enzymes	Proteins

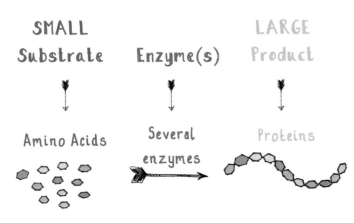

SEVERAL ENZYMES are involved in the synthesis of **proteins** from **amino acids**.

Glucose	Glycogen synthase	Glycogen

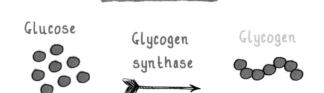

GLYCOGEN SYNTHASE synthesises **glycogen** (the carbohydrate used to store energy in animals) from **glucose**.

Fatty Acids & Glycerol	Several enzymes	Lipids

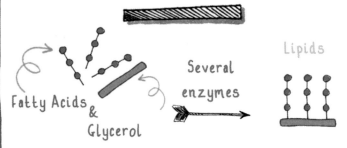

SEVERAL ENZYMES are involved in the synthesis of **lipids** from **fatty acids and glycerol**.

PROTEINS...

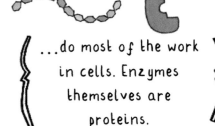

...do most of the work in cells. Enzymes themselves are proteins.

CARBOHYDRATES...

...such as glycogen and starch can be used to store energy.

LIPIDS...

...can also store energy and are important components of cell membranes.

TESTS FOR CARBOHYDRATES

BENEDICT'S REAGENT test for REDUCING SUGARS

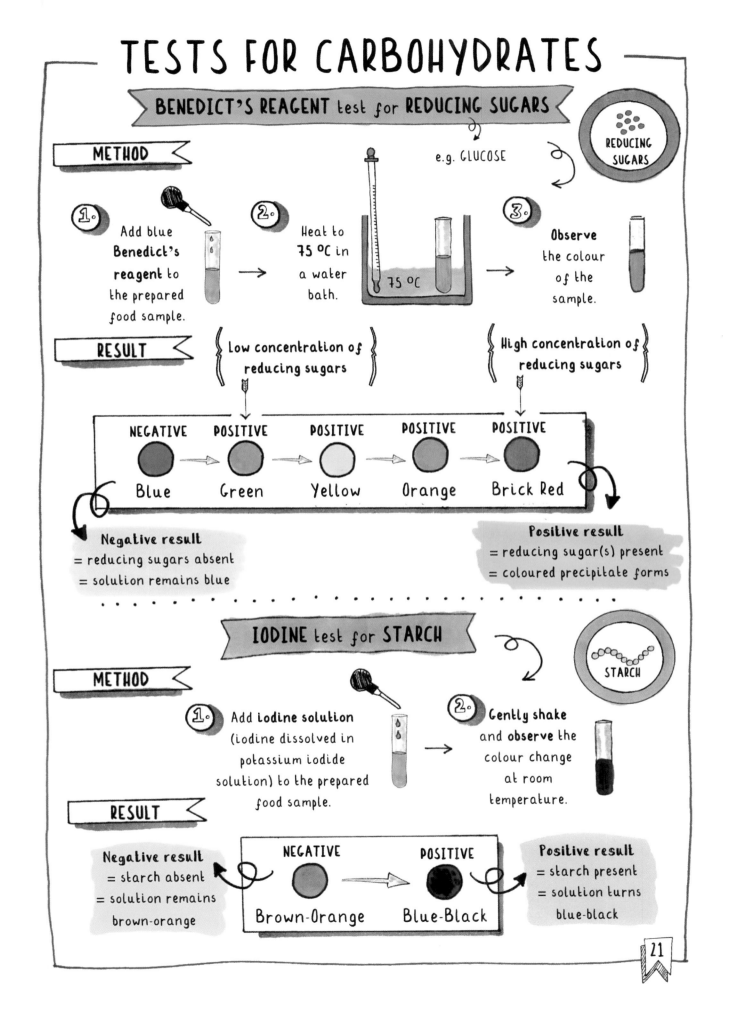

REDUCING SUGARS

e.g. GLUCOSE

METHOD

1. Add blue **Benedict's reagent** to the prepared food sample.

2. Heat to **75 °C** in a water bath.

75 °C

3. Observe the colour of the sample.

RESULT

{ Low concentration of reducing sugars }

{ High concentration of reducing sugars }

NEGATIVE	POSITIVE	POSITIVE	POSITIVE	POSITIVE
Blue	Green	Yellow	Orange	Brick Red

Negative result
= reducing sugars absent
= solution remains blue

Positive result
= reducing sugar(s) present
= coloured precipitate forms

IODINE test for STARCH

STARCH

METHOD

1. Add **iodine solution** (iodine dissolved in potassium iodide solution) to the prepared food sample.

2. **Gently shake** and **observe** the colour change at room temperature.

RESULT

Negative result
= starch absent
= solution remains brown-orange

NEGATIVE	POSITIVE
Brown-Orange	Blue-Black

Positive result
= starch present
= solution turns blue-black

21

TESTS FOR LIPIDS AND PROTEINS

EMULSION test for LIPIDS

LIPIDS

METHOD

1. Add **ethanol** to the prepared food sample.

2. Shake for 1 minute to dissolve the sample.

3. Pour the dissolved sample into **water**.

4. Observe the appearance of a creamy, fatty emulsion at room temperature.

RESULT

Negative result
= lipids absent
= no fatty emulsion

NEGATIVE	POSITIVE
No fatty emulsion	Creamy, fatty emulsion

Positive result
= lipid(s) present
= a fatty emulsion forms on the top of the solution
(the thicker the layer, the more lipid is present)

BIURET test for PROTEINS

PROTEINS

METHOD

1. Add 2-3 drops of **potassium hydroxide** solution to the prepared food sample.

2. Add some bright blue **copper (II) sulphate** solution.

3. Gently shake and **observe** the colour change at room temperature.

RESULT

Negative result
= proteins absent
= solution remains blue

NEGATIVE	POSITIVE
Blue	Purple

Positive result
= protein(s) present
= solution turns purple

ENERGY IN FOOD

CALORIMETRY → Burning food to measure how much energy it contains.

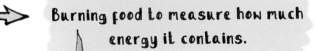

METHOD

1. Set up the equipment as shown in the diagram below. Measure and record the **starting temperature of the water** and the **mass of the dry food**.

☆ Mass of food (g) ···
☆ Start temp of water (°C) ···
☆ Final temp of water (°C) ···

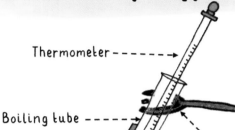

Thermometer - - - - - →

Boiling tube - - - - - →

Set volume of water - - - →

Foil insulation - - - - →

Clamp

Dry food
0.20g
Laboratory balance

NOTE! Use dry food e.g. pasta because it burns easily.

2. Set the food on **fire** and **immediately** place it **underneath the boiling tube** of water until the flame goes out.

Dried food on mounted needle

Bunsen burner

3. Set the **food on fire again** and hold it under the boiling tube of water. **Repeat** this process until the food no longer catches fire.

REPEAT ↻

4. Measure and record the **final temperature of the water**.

Fair Test

▷ To **prevent heat energy transferring directly from the Bunsen** burner to the water and impacting the result, keep the **Bunsen** burner **away from the water**.

▷ You can use **foil to insulate** the boiling tube. This will **minimise** the **loss of heat energy** from the water **to the environment**.

Foil ✓

ENERGY IN FOOD

What's going on?

▷ **Chemical energy in the food** (in the form of bonds) is **transferred** to the **water as heat energy**.

▷ The more energy in the food, the **more energy** will transfer and the **hotter** the water will get.

▷ Eventually when all of the **energy** in the food has been **used up** the food will **no longer catch fire**.

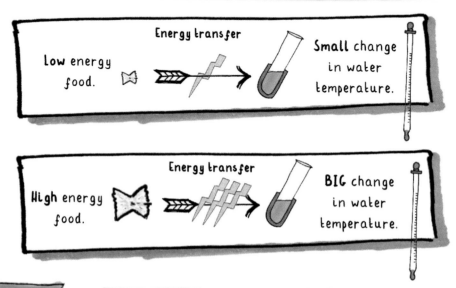

Low energy food.   Energy transfer   →   **Small** change in water temperature.

High energy food.   Energy transfer   →   **BIG** change in water temperature.

RESULT

STEP 1: HOW MANY JOULES?

Work out how much ENERGY (Joules, J) is in the piece of food that you have burned.

$$\text{Energy in food (Joules, J)} = \text{Mass of water (grams, g)} \times \text{Temperature increase of water (°C)} \times 4.2 \, (\text{J/g°C})$$

NOTE: Remember that $1 \, cm^3$ water $= 1 \, g$

STEP 2: HOW MANY JOULES PER GRAM?

Work out how much ENERGY would be in 1 gram of the food (Joules per gram, J/g).

$$\text{Energy per gram of food (Joules per gram, J/g)} = \text{Energy in food (J)} \div \text{Mass of food (g)}$$

Once you have this value, you can compare the energy content of different foods.

DIFFUSION

DIFFUSION ... is the **NET MOVEMENT** of **PARTICLES**, down a concentration gradient, from an area of **HIGH CONCENTRATION** to an area of **LOW CONCENTRATION**.

Only **small molecules** e.g oxygen, amino acids and glucose can diffuse across **cell membranes**. Large molecules need to be broken down by enzymes first!

NET movement of any particle from a **high** to **low** concentration.

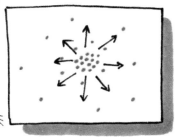

Diffusion happens **with or without a membrane**. ✓ ✗

NET movement of particles **DOWN** a **concentration gradient**.

Diffusion is a **PASSIVE PROCESS** i.e. it **does not require energy**. ✗

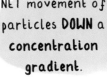
Diffusion happens when **particles naturally spread out** into more space.

Diffusion happens in **GASES** and **LIQUIDS**.

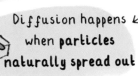

EXAMPLES

 IN THE LABORATORY...

Diffusion of potassium permanganate crystals in water.

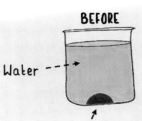

BEFORE   AFTER

Water - - - ▶

Lowest concentration

Potassium permanganate

Highest concentration

IMPORTANT!

During diffusion, **particles** move up and down the concentration gradient but **the NET movement of particles is DOWN the concentration gradient**. This means that **more particles move down** the concentration gradient, **than move up** the concentration gradient.

IN ANIMALS...

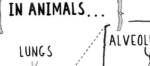

LUNGS

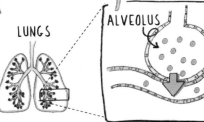

ALVEOLUS

BLOOD

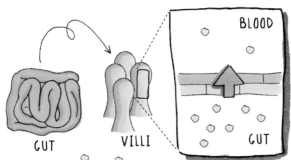

GUT   VILLI

BLOOD

GUT

In the **LUNGS**, **oxygen** diffuses from a high concentration in the **alveoli** to a low concentration in the **blood** circulating around the lungs.

Digested food diffuses from a high concentration in the **GUT** to a low concentration in the **blood** within the capillary of the villus.

25

OSMOSIS

... is the **NET MOVEMENT** of **WATER** molecules across a **PARTIALLY PERMEABLE MEMBRANE**, from an area of **HIGH CONCENTRATION** to an area of **LOW CONCENTRATION**.

This refers to the concentration of water molecules, not solute.

NET movement of water particles from a **high** to **low** concentration.

NET movement of water particles **DOWN** a concentration gradient.

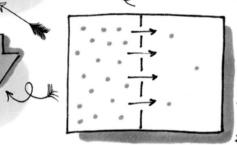

Osmosis is **NOT** the movement of solutes dissolved in water.

Osmosis happens **across** a **partially permeable membrane.** ✓

Osmosis is a **PASSIVE PROCESS** i.e. it **does not require energy.** ✗

Osmosis is a **special case of diffusion.**

Osmosis is specifically the movement of water particles.

EXAMPLE

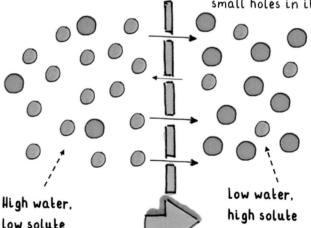

Partially permeable membrane: a membrane with very small holes in it. Only small molecules like water can pass through it.

High water, low solute concentrations.

Low water, high solute concentrations.

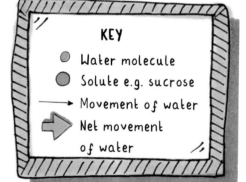

KEY
- Water molecule
- Solute e.g. sucrose
- → Movement of water
- Net movement of water

💧 Water molecules move in **both directions** across the membrane. However, the **solute** (e.g. sucrose) particles are **too large** to pass through the membrane.

💧 **More** water molecules **move down** the **concentration gradient** than move up the gradient. This means there is a **NET** movement of water towards the **lower water concentration** (the higher solute concentration).

ACTIVE TRANSPORT

ACTIVE TRANSPORT ...is the MOVEMENT OF PARTICLES AGAINST (or UP) a concentration gradient, from an area of LOW CONCENTRATION to an area of HIGH CONCENTRATION. This process requires ENERGY.

NET movement of particles from a low to high concentration.

Active transport happens **across a cell membrane.** ✓

NET movement of particles AGAINST (or UP) the concentration gradient.

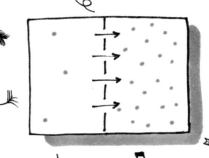

Think of a fish swimming **against the current. It would need a lot of energy!**

The **energy** needed for active transport is **produced during respiration** in the mitochondria.

Active transport works in the **opposite direction to diffusion and osmosis.**

Active transport is an **ACTIVE PROCESS** i.e. it requires energy.

EXAMPLES

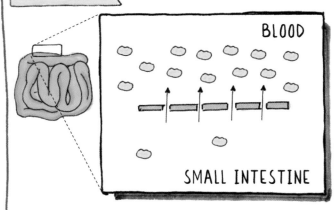

BLOOD

SMALL INTESTINE

ACTIVE TRANSPORT is needed when animals are starving. It ensures that **glucose** can be taken from a **low** concentration in the **intestine** to a **higher concentration** in the **blood.**

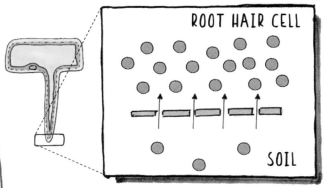

ROOT HAIR CELL

SOIL

In plants, **ACTIVE TRANSPORT** is needed for the uptake of **mineral ions.** Mineral ions are **actively transported** from **low concentrations** in the **soil** to **higher concentrations** in the **root hair cells.**

MOVEMENT OF MOLECULES

MOVEMENT TYPE	DIFFUSION	OSMOSIS	ACTIVE TRANSPORT
DIAGRAM	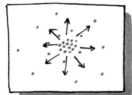	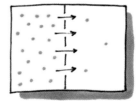	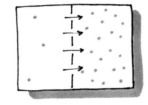
DIRECTION OF MOVEMENT	 High to low concentration. Down the concentration gradient.	 High to low concentration. Down the concentration gradient.	 Low to high concentration. Up (against) the concentration gradient.
MEMBRANE REQUIRED?	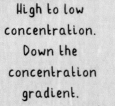 Can happen across a membrane but doesn't require one.	✓ Yes, a partially (semi-) permeable membrane e.g Visking tubing or a cell membrane.	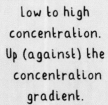 Yes, a cell membrane.
ENERGY REQUIRED?	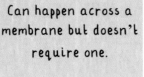 Passive - no energy required.	✗ Passive - no energy required.	 Active - energy required.
MOVEMENT OF?	 Any particle.	Water molecules.	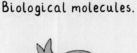 Biological molecules.
OTHER NOTES!	 Particles naturally spread out.	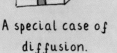 A special case of diffusion.	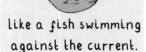 like a fish swimming against the current.

OSMOSIS PRACTICAL

INVESTIGATING OSMOSIS WITH SUCROSE SOLUTIONS AND POTATO.

METHOD

1.

Add a **different concentration of sucrose** (the solute) **solution** to each beaker. From pure water (0 M sucrose) to 1.0 M sucrose.

2.

Use a **cork borer** to cut 18 **identical pieces of potato** (1 cm in diameter). Separate the pieces into 6 **groups of 3**.

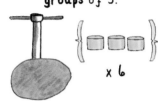

x 6

3.

Weigh each group of potato pieces and record the INITIAL MASS (grams, g) of each group.

4. Place **one group of potato pieces** into **each beaker**.

Highest water concentration   Pure water

Lowest water concentration

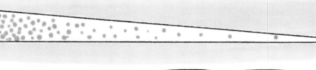

Lowest solute concentration

 0 M   0.2 M   0.4 M   0.6 M   0.8 M   1.0 M

Highest solute concentration

Concentration of Sucrose Solution (M)

5

Soak the potato pieces for a minimum of **40 minutes** then remove them from the sucrose solutions.

6.

Remove excess surface solution with a paper towel.

7.

Record the FINAL MASS (grams, g) of each group of potato pieces.

OSMOSIS PRACTICAL

Soak each group for the same amount of time.

HOW TO ENSURE A FAIR TEST:

Cut all pieces from the same potato.

Use the same drying method.

Use the same size potato pieces.

RESULT — CALCULATE THE PERCENTAGE CHANGE IN MASS

Work out the change in mass as a percentage of the initial mass.

$$\text{Percentage Change in Mass (\%)} = \frac{\text{Final mass (g)} - \text{Initial mass (g)}}{\text{Initial mass (g)}} \times 100$$

NOTE

The **percentage change in mass** allows you to compare groups with different **initial masses**.

EXAMPLE

The **initial mass** of a group of potato pieces was 10.4 g. The **final mass** was 11.6 g. Calculate the **percentage change in mass**.

$$\frac{11.6 - 10.4}{10.4} \times 100 = 11.5\%$$

PLOT YOUR RESULTS — EXAMPLE

Potato **gains mass** because the water concentration **inside** the potato cells is **lower than** the concentration of pure water/sucrose solution. **There is a net movement of water by osmosis INTO the potato cells.**

No gain in potato mass because the concentration of water inside the potato cells is **equal to** that of the sucrose solution. **There is no net movement of water.**

Potato **loses mass** because the water concentration **inside** the potato cells is **higher than** the concentration of water in the sucrose solution. **There is a net movement of water by osmosis OUT of the potato cells.**

(Graph: y-axis "Percentage Mass Change (%)" from -20 to 20; x-axis "Concentration of Sucrose Solution (M)" marked 0.2, 0.4, 0.6, 0.8, 1.0)

THE END...

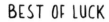

BEST OF LUCK

For updates and freebies!
Follow:
@doctormeclever

If you'd like to take a photo of your notes and
progress tracker, I'd love to see!
Just share online, tag me (@doctormeclever)
and use #doctormeclever.

WWW.DOCTORMECLEVER.COM